The Throws and Take-downs of

Freestyle Wrestling

Geoff Thompson

SUMMERSDALE

Summersdale Publishers Ltd
46 West Street
Chichester
West Sussex
PO19 1RP
United Kingdom

www.summersdale.com

Printed and bound in Great Britain.

ISBN 1 84024 028 8

First edit by Kerry Thompson.

Photographs by David W. Monks, member of the Master Photographers' Association
Snappy Snaps Portrait Studio
7 Cross Cheaping
Coventry
CV1 1HF

About the author

Geoff Thompson has written over 20 books and is known worldwide for his bestselling autobiography, *Watch My Back*, about his nine years working as a nightclub doorman. He currently has a quarter of a million books in print. He holds the rank of 6th Dan black belt in Japanese karate, 1st Dan in judo and is also qualified to senior instructor level in various other forms of wrestling and martial arts. He has several scripts for stage and screen in development with Destiny Films.

He has published articles for *GQ* magazine, and has also been featured in *FHM*, *Maxim*, *Arena*, *Front* and *Loaded* magazines, and has appeared many times on mainstream television. Geoff is currently a contributing editor for *Men's Fitness* magazine.

Geoff first learned freestyle wrestling at Birmingham Wrestling Club under Jim Ault. He also trained with USA champion Khris Wheelan and studied basic catch wrestling under Dave Turton.

Thanks to Jim Ault and all the members of the Birmingham Wrestling Club.

For a free colour brochure of Geoff Thompson's
books and videos please ring the
24-hour hotline on 02476 431100 or write to:

Geoff Thompson Ltd
PO Box 307
Coventry
CV3 2YP

www.geoffthompson.com
www.summersdale.com

Contents

Freestyle Wrestling

Introduction

Welcome to the throws and take-downs of freestyle wrestling, thank you for taking the time to read this book. You are probably well aware of the fact that grappling and ground fighting are the current favourites in the world of martial arts, and much has been said of late about the grappling arts. They seem to be experiencing something of a revival, a well-earned and long awaited renaissance. Between 1899 and 1914, proper wrestling (rather than 'show wrestling') was huge, so much so that the period was called the Golden Age of Wrestling. People like Hackeschmidt, Pojelo, Stalislauz Sabisko and the Great Turk actually made their fortunes in the wrestling rings of Europe. The wrestlers of the day were revered, much like the pop stars of today. The Golden Era lost its sheen and all but died off just before, some say because of, the Great War, only to be revived and reborn as show grappling post-war. There was never a better time for wrestling and now, at long last, people are starting to seek it out once again. It is a great art and my hope is that this time around it will stay for good as a vital part of our martial art heritage.

Perhaps because grappling is not quite so aesthetically pleasing as some of the other arts due to its unembellished demeanour, its devastating potency has consequently been hidden from the untrained eye; people are naturally drawn to the more superfluously spectacular arts that are splashed across our cinema screens. However, the world of combat, and more specifically the world of martial art, has now evolved and many of these so-called spectacular arts have failed to cut the mustard, they have fallen well short of being effective in an arena (the street) that does not suffer mistakes gladly. The gorgeous systems, as I like to call them, are all shine and no substance. The fundamental movements of the grappling arts, so often ignored because of the Plain Jane factor, have come to the fore and proved themselves worthy of the name 'martial'.

Freestyle Wrestling

The rise of the UFC (Ultimate Fight Competition) – cage fighting, reality combat and extreme fighting – has done us all a favour in that they have pointed out to all but the blind the gaping holes in the martial armoury of most contemporary arts. Now, everybody suddenly wants to join a grappling club. This is great in theory because we need to be competent in all ranges of combat so that any leaks can be sealed. The problems start to arise when people abandon their old arts in favour of the new and to the detriment of all the other ranges. Grappling without punching and kicking is just as limited as kicking and punching without grappling. I can understand this to a degree, ground grappling is the flavour right now and everyone (myself included) has been seduced by it. Grappling is the prodigal son of the martial arts that has returned home after so long. And because of the success of grapplers in the UFC style tournaments everyone is desperate to make up for lost time and fill his or her sack with the much needed and oft neglected art of ground fighting. And so they should. I've been trying to tell people this for the last ten years.

Having worked as a nightclub doorman for nine years I always knew that grappling was a vital part of the martial armoury. But learning grappling to the exclusion of all other ranges is suicide and this is where the problems begin. Whilst it is important, even imperative, to include grappling on the curriculum we should never neglect the punching and kicking of our base systems. Especially punching because in a real fight, where the chip shop is your arena, the art of punching is your best chance (and often your only choice) for survival. Go to the ground in this arena and even strangers will kick you in the head when you're down. They can't help themselves' it's human nature. Mix alcohol and blood and stir in a bit of peer pressure and nice people turn into the most despicable creatures. My point is this, what we are ending up with now are martial artists who are training only in grappling, they are abandoning their other disciplines such as punching and kicking so as to concentrate all of their time and energy on the art of floor fighting. This will leave them impaired as martial artists. The fighter that has become a great grappler (because he has watched and was inspired by

Freestyle Wrestling

the reality tapes) finds himself being punched out in the bar or kicked to pieces outside the chippy.

It's important to grapple, imperative even, but it is also vital that we stay in context. Grapple yes, I'd even insist upon it, but never neglect the other ranges that make to complete the armoury. If one range is neglected all ranges suffer because when you need your skills to save your life you may be judged on the strength of your weakest range. You are, as they say, only as strong as your weakest link.

Equally, with the ground fighting phenomenon there has been little or no notice taken of throwing techniques. Neil Adams always told me that your groundwork was only as strong as your tachi waza. If you are thrown or taken to the floor and end in a bad position you might never get out of it, a good player – hell, even a road digger – won't let up once he has the advantage. In the dojo you might lose the contest, you can live with that; in the street it may be your life you lose if your opponent punches your head into the tarmac while you are on your back. Most people start their ground fighting from a neutral position. Both fighters with an equal start. Outside the chippy, when the fight goes live, there is no such neutrality and you very much have to make the best of what you are given, that is unless you are the one who controls the take-down. Do you ever watch the prowess of ground fighters and think, 'It's alright fighting on the floor but how do you get there safely from standing?' Me too, that's why I decided to write these books on the art of taking an opponent off his feet with a practised throwing technique.

In this volume we are looking at the throws and take-downs of freestyle wrestling. Having studied this system to instructor level I can vouch for the potency and dynamism of this much-underrated art. When I was training in Birmingham with the freestyle wrestlers I was awed both by their fighting prowess and their gentleness. On my first night at the club I thought, rather arrogantly I might add, that I might do OK; I was strong, I had a lot of real fight experience and I had dabbled in grappling on and off for a number of years. When Jim, the

Freestyle Wrestling

lovely instructor at the club, asked us to choose a partner I went for the biggest guy in the place. I have to tell you that he pulled me around like I was a baby. He was the European heavyweight champion and he was ******* good. I have never felt so humbled. At one stage he actually picked me up above his head. He could have slammed me down and buried me into the mat quite easily, but he didn't, this gentle giant placed me back on to my feet so that I could have another try. I was awed by the gentleness of this man and the memory has stuck with me ever since.

There are some excellent people at freestyle wrestling, people a lot better than I am; I would advice and recommend that you seek them out and get a bit of one-on-one training, there really is no substitute.

As I have said in all of the books in this series, don't make the throws and take-downs the be all and end all. The same goes with the ground fighting, on its own it is not much use, you need to combine it with all the other physical and psychological ranges otherwise your jigsaw is going to have vital pieces missing.

A word of warning too: many opponents in a live scenario will not allow you to throw them cleanly, they will panic-grip you like their very lives depend upon it and drag you to the floor with them. If you don't know how to fight on the floor then you are up shit creek.

Don't rely on this book (or any other for that matter) to teach you, it must be used in combination with a good class or partner, there is nothing like a real opponent to perfect the physical technique. Join a good wrestling club. I'd go as far as to say that it cannot be learned properly by book alone. Learn the fundamentals of the technique, then put it under the pressure of a non-compliant partner to perfect. Once you can use the technique on someone that doesn't want to be thrown, then you know you have got it off. Learn to do it under pressure, too much compliance in training weakens you and prevents you from developing the right muscles or the right technique to make it happen for real. Compliance is only of use when first learning the fundamentals of a technique, once learned, an opponent should offer 100 per cent resistance and he should also try to throw you. There is nothing like the feel of taking a throw when you know that you opponent has done everything in his power to stop you. It builds your confidence no end. You need to fight, you need the free sparring, taking the randori (free-fighting or sparring) out of a system is effectively taking the claws and teeth from a tiger.

I wish you the very best of luck with your practise and thank you for taking the time to read the book.

Chapter One
Balance, Stance, Grip

Lets start with the base. Balance is imperative, you can know every throw in the book but it won't help if you haven't got the balance and stance right. You will have little joy throwing an opponent and you'll be easily thrown when your balance is off. Balance can be developed in technique work but it will only really come together when you get on the mat and have a few fights. You soon learn balance when everyone in the club is trying to flatten the world with your back. When I first started training in Birmingham my balance was way out. As a consequence I was on the floor more times than the cleaner's mop. I got tired of climbing back to my feet. But that was good, that's how I learned. If you are in a class where you are not getting thrown then you are in the wrong class. It's how you grow; and as I said, there is no better incentive to learn than being thrown around like a paper bag in a storm night after night.

Freestyle Wrestling

Because freestyle wrestling allows attacks above and below the waist (in Greco they only allow attacks above the waist) the players tend to stand very low, certainly lower than they would if they were practising Greco or judo. Because they are crouched so low many of the traditional throws, as seen in judo for instance, are very hard to pull off. Subsequently the freestyle wrestler tends to aim below the waist, specifically at the legs, with the majority of his attacks.

While fighting for a grip, good players usually work in a low straddle stance, only moving into the wedge position (left or right lead 45-degree stance) when preparing to attack.

Freestyle Wrestling

Holding this stance can be very tiring on the thighs, but that's why the wrestlers are so well conditioned: it is worth the pain. These are just the fundamentals; it's best to practise the right way from the very beginning; if you can get yourself into a good club – even better. I do hope that this book will act as an appetiser for you to really get into this fantastic art. Of all the martial arts I have practised, I'd have to say that the grappling arts have been the most satisfying.

In all books of this genre I work on the presumption that you are working from a left lead stance (this can be reversed of course). This being the case, you should stand in a small 45-degree wedge stance with knees bent and relaxed.

In this position your weight is directly over a point just behind the heel of your front foot. The knees are flexed and your back is essentially upright and almost perpendicular to the floor. The head is up and in direct line with the spine. The shoulders are parallel to the floor.

Freestyle Wrestling

In all forms of fighting, balance is everything. The wedge stance maximises your balance so that you can shoot in and throw your opponent. It is also pivotal to have your balance right so that you can react quickly when your opponent tries to shoot in and throw you. The only time that the stance should change is when you enter to take a throw or defend a throw. After you attack – or are attacked – immediately revert back to the stance. If you successfully throw the opponent you have the option to follow him down to ground or stay on your feet. In the sporting arena you would probably follow the opponent to the floor and fight from there. On the street, going to the floor would not be recommended – staying vertical would. Your choice.

Grip around the opponent's right triceps with your left hand and grip the back of the opponent's neck with your right.

Freestyle Wrestling

This is the basic stance and grip to take when looking for a throw. As the play becomes more advanced you will have to fight for your grip, an opponent will not just allow you to take advantage. Good grip fighters spend a great proportion of the match fighting for the dominant grip. When I wrestle I aim to dominate the grip right from the off. Once I have a dominant grip it is pretty easy for me to take a throw and very difficult for my opponent to do anything other than defend. Grip is so important. If you get a chance to look at my videos of the throws and take-downs this is demonstrated very clearly. It took me nearly a year to get the grips right. Once they fell into place my whole game improved no end. When entering for a throw the grip will naturally change according to which throw you attempt.

In a street scenario you rarely get to choose the grip you start with, though once you perfect the grip work you can change your holds at will. Initially you may have to take the grip that is available and then, if it is not one that suits you, change it for one that does. Once the grips and throws have been mastered you will be able to take an opponent over from any grip and from any position. For now though, be content to work with the fundamentals until such time as you feel more competent.

Good grip work can enable light players to control and destroy heavy players. It may seem unlikely but, honestly, when I was at the wrestling club some of the smaller players tied me in knots with superior technique, even though I often weighed several stone more than them.

In the street you are very unlikely to face an expert grappler, so for this arena you just need to make sure that you can hold your nerve and apply very basic techniques very well. This comes from heavy drilling and supervision, also pressure training where you are pushed to your physical and mental limitations.

Grip and stance in place you are now equipped to break the balance of the opponent and set him up for a throw. On a

Freestyle Wrestling

street level we are unlikely to encounter anyone with great balance although they may have an innate instinct to stay vertical – no one is just going to let you throw them. On a dojo level however, you will be working with players trained in the art of not being thrown and a good wrestler is very difficult to off-balance and harder still to throw. I watched Kevin Darkus (USA champion) fighting at the Birmingham club with one of the local internationals one evening. I was awed. It was like poetry in motion. Kevin looked like a gymnast as he twisted and turned his way out of throws that seemed impossible to escape. Good wrestlers like Kevin are hugely flexible and, to be honest, almost impossible to throw (unless they let you, which they sometimes do). Similarly, when I fought with Neil Adams in judo I found it impossible to even get a grip on him unless he let me (which, again, he did). His defence and grip work were set at an incredible pitch.

Breaking the opponent's balance is the precursor to throwing him. In fact, with a player of equal skill you are very unlikely to throw him at all without breaking balance first.

Basically, breaking the opponent's balance is pretty much the same in all grappling styles; you employ pulling or pushing actions, or you attempt to feign one throw to open him up for another.

You can break the opponent's balance by pushing or pulling the opponent to the left rear, directly behind, to the right rear or directly to his right or left. Alternatively you can pull the opponent directly towards you, to your left or right rear or directly to the right or left. You can also pull him downward. Any one of these actions will force the opponent to move, hopefully out of stance and off balance, and when he does you can execute a throw.

Another opportunity to off balance an opponent and throw him is when he makes an attack (a throw or punch, for example). As he makes his entry you take advantage of his stance change to take him over. All throwing actions rely on feeling and going with the energy. This is something that has to be felt. It is difficult to relate it as clearly as I'd like via the pages of a book.

Stiff Arming

Stiff arming is recognised in most forms of grappling and, to be honest, it is really hard when you are first learning to get past a stiff armer who is frightened to death of being thrown.

Freestyle Wrestling

It usually occurs with over-muscular, strong (but with no technique), less skilful or very scared opponents. These are often the exact types you will meet in a street encounter. They literally hold you to the spot with their strength, normally out of sheer panic. They don't even attack or defend, they just hold on, and if you are not used to dealing with them they can kill your technique dead. Dealing with stiff armers requires good grip work and a good sense of flow; use their strength against them by going with the flow of energy. In a street encounter it's a little simpler: just whack them in the head (or kick them in the shin or groin) and it distracts their strength away from their grip and to the area that you attack. This allows you a way through. In old judo this was called 'blow before throw'. You would use a strike, or blow, to open the opponent up for a throw.

Obviously in most sport-grappling this would be frowned upon so it goes without saying that you should refrain from such behaviour (unless of course the referee isn't looking). The blow before throw will break the balance of the stiff armer, creating a window of opportunity, then you can bang in the throw.

In the street you generally encounter fighters with little or no clothing to grab (nudist camps are a nightmare I have to tell you, though in these circumstances there are other things you can grab to aid the throw. Say no more. Maybe I should do a book on the art of fighting nudes? *Bare-naked Boxing* perhaps or *Self-defence Against the Streaker*? The videos would go a treat. Perhaps not! I am going off on a tangent again).

Where was I? Oh yes. Greco and freestyle come into their own on the street because the wrestling type throws use the opponent's limbs as opposed to the clothing to make the throw. From my experience of working with several systems of grappling, the wrestling take-downs work magnificently in the street for this reason. They need no appendage other than natural hooks like the arms, neck, waist and legs. Some of the Greco snatches and freestyle leg take-downs come into their own in these scenarios.

Grips

Here are a few of the grips used in freestyle and Greco-Roman wrestling.

Note: Never intertwine your fingers, when you try to pull them apart it is very easy to dislocate your fingers or knuckles.

Grab Finger Grip

Grab the four fingers of your left hand with the four fingers of your right hand. Lock them by closing your fists together firmly. Pull on all four fingers of both hands at the same time to ensure the lock.

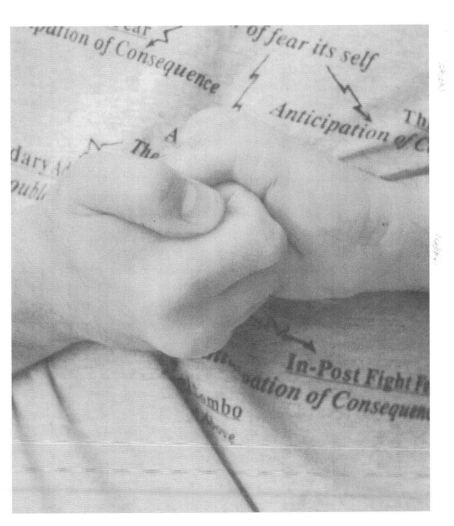

Wrist Grip

Grab your left wrist with your right hand (or vice versa) with
your thumb and forefinger around your left wrist.

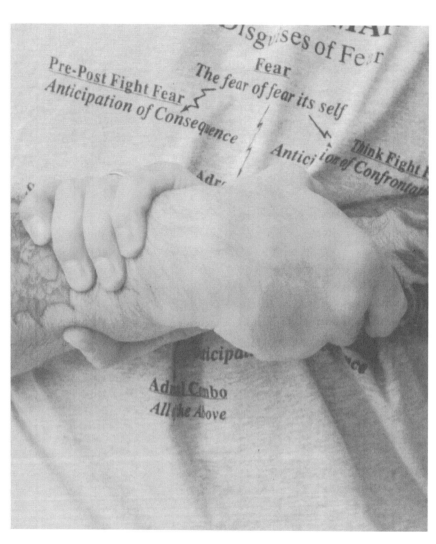

Grab Back of Hand and Wrist

Grab the blade side of your left wrist with your right hand. Your two smallest fingers should be around the wrist, the bigger fingers on the blade side of the hand. Your thumb should be on the same side as the fingers.

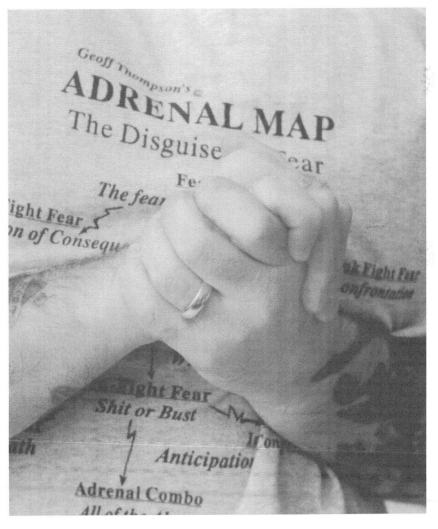

Palm to Palm Grip

Place your left palm on your right palm and clasp both hands

around each other.

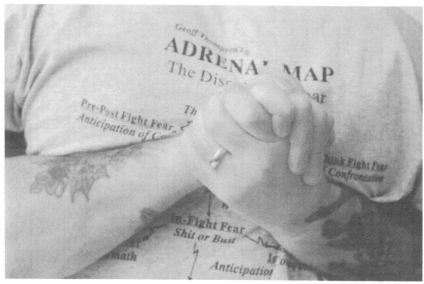

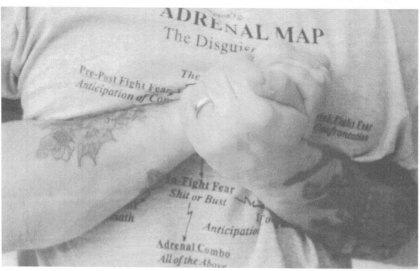

Palm to Bicep Grip

Grab your right bicep with your left hand; bend the left arm

to make the grip or lock strong. This lock is used especially

for face or arm bars.

Freestyle Wrestling

It is important that you have a pull around with an opponent (preferably lots of different opponents) to get used to balance, grip and entries for the throws; the more time you are on the mat the better.

Chapter Two
The Cross Buttock

The cross buttock appears in nearly all forms of stand up wrestling and the technique differs very little from one style to the next. The main difference in freestyle is the fact that the throw is usually taken from a headlock as opposed to a waist grip, and of course there is no clothing to aid in the throw because the wrestlers wear only a leotard.

Where it also varies is in the fact that the wrestlers over-commit their bottom when executing the throw. With the judo and ju-jitsu people, the bottom or hips tend to be square with the opponent's lower abdomen, and the throw is taken over the hip. Wrestlers, however, prefer to push the hip past the lower abdomen to the other side of the opponent and then throw them over the small of the back (see illustrations). Personally I feel uncomfortable with both, the hip throw does not suit me at all, but that doesn't mean that it will not work for you. It certainly does for many of my training partners.

Freestyle Wrestling

When I employed this technique on the door, and I did a few times, it was always the version from the headlock that I used.

Grab the opponent in a headlock position and turn your back and buttocks into his lower stomach and past centre. Bend deeply at the knees and, using your right headlock grip, pull the opponent over the small of your back and slam him to the floor.

Freestyle Wrestling

If the opponent locks off here and you can't throw him over your back then try dropping quickly to your knees and throwing him from here. The momentum from the drop itself is usually enough to take him over.

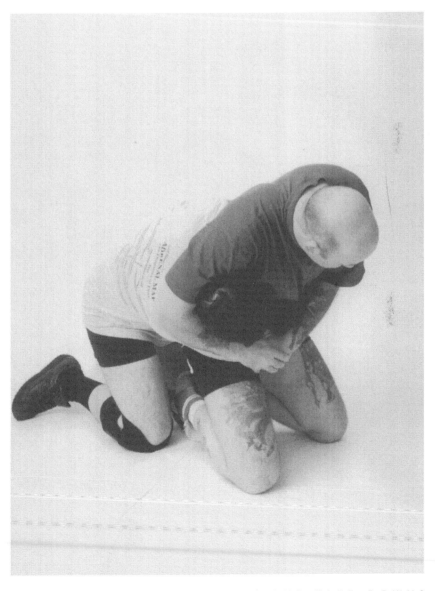

Freestyle Wrestling

Alternatively, if the opponent locks you off and you are struggling to take the throw, prop your right leg across the front of the opponent's right leg and change the hip throw to a body drop. The transition from one to the other should be very quick and you should drop your levels slightly so as to take the opponent off balance.

This throw can also be taken with a waist grip as opposed to a head grip. Simply wrap your right arm around the opponent's waist and turn your back and buttocks into his lower stomach and past centre. Bend deeply at the knees and pull the opponent over the small of your back and slam him to the floor.

Again, if the opponent locks off here and you can't throw him over your back then try dropping quickly to your knees and throwing him from here.

Freestyle Wrestling

Yet another alternative to aid the throw is to take the grip under the opponent's right armpit: in the usual way turn your back and buttocks into his lower stomach and past centre. Bend deeply at the knees and pull the opponent, using your right headlock grip, over the small of your back and slam him to the floor.

Freestyle Wrestling

If the opponent resists the throw by spreading his legs and pulling backwards you can counter his counter by going with the energy and thrust your right leg between his legs and behind his right leg, using it to trip him backwards. As you trip him, drive him back by pushing off your support leg.

Back view:

Freestyle Wrestling

If he reacts to stop your initial hip throw by forcing his bodyweight slightly to the front, you can finish the throw by adding a sweeping harai goshi type movement with your right leg. Sweep your right leg up and to the side of his right thigh and sweep him over and on to his back.

Chapter Three
The Flying Mare (Shoulder Throw)

The shoulder throw, or flying mare, is another technique common in all forms of vertical grappling arts. The unique thing about the un-jacketed wrestling systems is that they take the throw without the use of an appendage, using only the limbs of the opponent.

Grab the opponent's right wrist with your left hand. Turn your back into the opponent's belly and thrust your right arm high under his right armpit. Bend at the knees so that you are below the opponent's centre of gravity and then straighten your legs, pulling him on to and over your shoulder. Use your right and left arm to pull him over and slam him to the floor.

Freestyle Wrestling

The Flying Mare (Shoulder Throw)

Freestyle Wrestling

If the opponent locks off here and you can't throw him, then try dropping quickly to your knees and throwing him from here. The momentum from the drop itself is usually enough to take him over.

The Flying Mare (Shoulder Throw)

Alternatively, if the opponent locks you off and you are struggling to take the throw, prop your right leg across the front of the opponent's right leg and change the shoulder throw to a body drop. The transition from one to the other should be very quick and you should drop your levels slightly so as to take the opponent off balance.

Freestyle Wrestling

If the opponent resists the throw by spreading his legs and pulling backwards you can counter his counter by going with the energy and thrust your right leg between his legs and behind his right leg, using it to trip him backwards. As you trip him, drive him back by pushing off your support leg. Be sure to lock his right arm off with your left when you take the throw.

Back view:

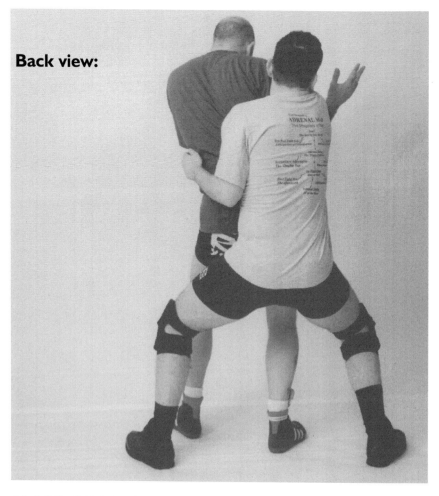

The Flying Mare (Shoulder Throw)

Freestyle Wrestling

If he reacts to stop your initial throw by forcing his bodyweight slightly to the front, you can finish the throw by adding a sweep with your right leg. Sweep your right leg up and to the side of his right thigh and then sweep him over and on to his back.

The Flying Mare (Shoulder Throw)

Another alternative to him blocking the initial throw is to take an outside reaping throw. Twist your body quickly to face the opponent, hooking your right leg on the outside of his right leg and sweeping him backwards with an outside reap.

Chapter Four
Standing Arm Roll

The standing arm roll is a typical freestyle (or Greco) throw, again utilising the opponent's limbs to the full. This kind of technique is more applicable to the street due to the fact that we rarely get anything of any substance, other than the limbs, to grab and use as an appendage.

Grab the opponent's right wrist with your left hand, turn into him and lash your right arm right across the front of his face and over his right arm, pulling it tightly under your armpit. As you pull the opponent forward, bend your left leg and drive your right leg in front of his right ankle and body drop him over your leg by pulling hard with your right and left arms.

Freestyle Wrestling

Chapter Five
Double Leg Pick-up

Leg throws are the mainstream of freestyle wrestling and if there is one thing that they are famous for, it is the explosive and devastating shoot leg attacks.

With the double leg pick-up or take down, start by thrusting the opponent's arms up and above your head as he reaches to grip. Lunge forward and low with your left leg. Wrap your arms around the upper thighs of the opponent, your head to his left (or right) thigh. As you pick him off the floor, turn directly behind you to your left and simultaneously wrap your left arm around his waist, tipping the opponent's head towards the ground. Slam him to the mat.

Freestyle Wrestling

Double Leg Pick-up

If the opponent reacts to your pick-up by reaching over your back, continue through with your right leg and wrap your left heel behind his left leg and heel trip him to his back.

This, and of course all the throws that you want to make your own, needs to be drilled as a separate throw and then as secondary throws to counter the opponent's reaction should the first one fail. If you drill the throws enough, eventually you will automatically react and go with whatever energy the opponent gives you.

Chapter Six
Single Leg Take-down

What is important in the early stages of learning a throw is to get the basic mechanics of the take-down. Later the set up, reacting to energy or creating and then reacting to energy, becomes more important. This is especially so when fighting against another skilled wrestler. In the street scenario, which I am more concerned with, the set up is not as important as the mechanics of the throw, because outside the novice wrestler will automatically give you the energy for one throw or another. In the gym it becomes a game of chess, often working several moves ahead of yourself at all times using draws and feigns and often making sacrifices to create the energy for a decisive take-down.

Single leg take-downs are my favourite in the freestyle system and, although they do expend a lot of energy, they work very well.

Freestyle Wrestling

From the bicep control grip, lung forward and low with your left (or right) leg and pick the opponent's right leg up at the back of the knee. Allow your right hand to slide to the back of the opponent's heel and place your left palm on his thigh. Pull the leg back with the right hand as you force down and around to your left with the left palm to take the opponent over.

Freestyle Wrestling

If the opponent reacts by leaning forward and grabbing under your left arm, shoot behind him by bringing your right leg to the rear and force the opponent over on to his belly.

Freestyle Wrestling

Again, drill the techniques independently and then in combination until you can feel the right energy for the right throw.

Chapter Seven
The Fireman's Carry

The fireman's carry can be employed either standing or kneeling. I will start by demonstrating the standing version and then go on to the kneeling version and the secondary attacks to the opponent's expected defence.

Duck under the opponent's arms and drive your right leg between his legs. Crouch so that your legs are at maximum bend and your back is still straight; simultaneously wrap your right arm around the back of the opponent's right knee (or alternatively fire the arm between his leg and up his back). Straighten your legs and stand up with the opponent on your back, and as you do so, slam him on to his back.

Freestyle Wrestling

An alternative to rolling the opponent over your shoulder is to throw him either directly forward, over your head and on to his back, or directly backwards on to his back. Either will suffice.

For the kneeling fireman's lift the entry is the same. Duck under the opponent's arms and drive your right leg between his legs, wrapping your right arm around the back of his left knee. Land between the opponent's legs, on your knees and facing your own left. Your back should be poker-straight. Tip and roll the opponent over your left shoulder and on to his back.

Freestyle Wrestling

If the opponent reacts to the kneeling fireman's lift by sprawling, tighten the grip that you have on his right arm and barrel roll to your left so that the opponent is thrown on to his back.

Side view:

Conclusion

That concludes the throws and take-downs of freestyle wrestling. I hope that you have enjoyed and learned from this text. As I have stated in all of the books in this series, this is not a comprehensive text on freestyle throws and take-downs, neither is it meant to be representative of the whole freestyle system; it is simply a collection of the throws and take-downs from this Olympic art that I like and find most effective. Hopefully, at the very least, it will encourage you to seek out a wrestling club near you so that you can study the art in greater detail. There is no substitute for a good teacher and a club full of willing training partners.

As with anything worth its salt, these techniques will not just magically happen because you have read a book on wrestling; they will need conscientious and arduous practise to make them your own. And if you wish to employ them in reality combat (the ring of the street) then you will surely have to make them just that.

Freestyle Wrestling

I should also mention that, in regards to a real encounter in the street, I recommend flight above fight. Always walk away rather than fight if the circumstances allow. Violence is not the answer in the majority of cases and a physical response should only be undertaken if no other option is open to you. I always try to avoid confrontational situations as much as possible. I employ verbal dissuasion if I can't escape, and loophole or posture if dissuasion has failed me. Having been in hundreds of affrays in my lifetime I can categorically tell you that it is a stronger, braver and more confident man that walks away.

If this is all impossible and an attack is imminent then don't wait to be attacked, attack first and then escape. Your main artillery in this circumstance is nearly always your hands (punching or striking) and any form of close range grappling should be relegated to being a support system. For more information on the other ranges of combat and the realities of street combat please refer to my other texts, some of which are advertised in the back of this book.

Thank you for taking the time to read this book and good luck in your search for better defence.

God bless.

Geoff Thompson 2001

The Throws and Take-Downs of Sombo

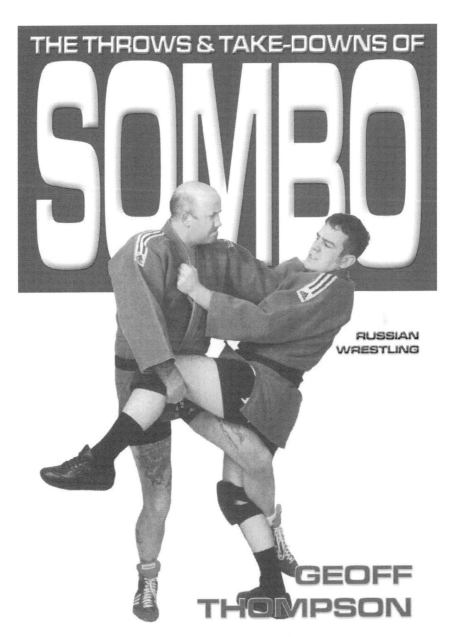

THE THROWS & TAKE-DOWNS OF

SOMBO

RUSSIAN
WRESTLING

GEOFF
THOMPSON

SUMMERSDALE

The Throws and Take-Downs of Greco-Roman Wrestling

THE THROWS & TAKE-DOWNS OF

GRECO-ROMAN WRESTLING

GEOFF
THOMPSON

SUMMERSDALE

The Throws and Take-Downs of Judo

THE THROWS & TAKE-DOWNS OF JUDO

GEOFF THOMPSON

SUMMERSDALE

Geoff Thompson's autobiography,
Watch My Back

GEOFF THOMPSON

WATCH MY BACK

'I train for the first shot
– it's all I need.'

'LENNIE MCLEAN HAD THE BRAWN, DAVE COURTNEY HAD THE
CHARM, BUT GEOFF THOMPSON IS IN A CLASS OF HIS OWN.' FHM

www.geoffthompson.com

www.summersdale.com